To my wife Renee, the librarian,

and to my two boys, Griffin and Max,

you can achieve anything!

When I go to the library,

I follow all the rules.

I don't speak out loud,

and I don't talk to girls.

When I bring a book home,

my mom always asks,

"What did you get, honey?

Is it a book full of fun facts?"

I hold it up proudly,

and I say with a smile,

"It's a book about my favorite dinosaur,

the Tyrannosaurus Rex!"

I read about tigers,

and mountains,

and things that jump high.

I've even read books

that make me want to fly!

And when I feel there

is nothing new to read,

I know it's ok,

because I have a secret

that is great indeed!

You see, my mom is a librarian,

and she has superpowers.

She knows Dewey Decimal

and how to catalog for hours.

She bounds from bookshelf to bookshelf,

not missing a step.

She has books from Blume to Seuss
and even Sendak.

My friends always ask me,

"How do you know so much?"

I just grin from ear to ear,

and tell them, "It's just luck."

But just between you and me,

I'll say it again.

It's because of my secret,

my mom is a librarian.

Made in the USA
Monee, IL
19 February 2022

90738017R00019